Organizational Change i

ORGANIZATIONAL

CHANGE IN 100 DAYS

A Fast Forward Guide

Elspeth J. Murray and

Peter R. Richardson

OXFORD
UNIVERSITY PRESS

2003

OXFORD
UNIVERSITY PRESS

Oxford   New York

Auckland   Bangkok   Buenos Aires   Cape Town   Chennai
Dar es Salaam   Delhi   Hong Kong   Istanbul   Karachi   Kolkata
Kuala Lumpur   Madrid   Melbourne   Mexico City   Mumbai   Nairobi
São Paulo   Shanghai   Taipei   Tokyo   Toronto

Copyright © 2003 by Oxford University Press, Inc.

Published by Oxford University Press, Inc.
198 Madison Avenue, New York, New York, 10016

www.oup.com

Oxford is a registered trademark of Oxford University Press

Library of Congress Cataloging-in-Publication Data
Murray, Elspeth J., 1961–
    Organizational change in 100 days : a fast forward guide / Elspeth J. Murray and Peter
R. Richardson.
    p. cm.
    A guide to the author's Fast forward. 2002.
    ISBN 0-19-515312-X (pbk.)
    1. Organizational change. 2. Strategic planning. I. Title: Organizational change in one
hundred days. II. Title: Fast forward guide. III. Richardson, Peter R., 1947– IV. Murray,
Elspeth J., 1961– Fast forward. V. Title.

HD58.8 .M8753 2003
658.4'02—dc21   2002034903

9 8 7 6 5 4 3 2 1

Printed in the United States of America
on acid-free paper

Contents

This Guide outlines a way of thinking and
an approach for implementing deep organizational
change. It is to be used in conjunction with
Fast Forward: Organizational Change in 100 Days,
by Elspeth J. Murray and Peter R. Richardson
(New York: The Oxford University Press, 2002).

Introduction

This Guide has been created to assist executives in thinking systematically about their organizational change activities, in diagnosing the effectiveness of these initiatives, and in developing specific actions to improve the process and accelerate the pace of change in their organizations. The starting point for users of the Guide is the recognition that a new strategy or major change is required for your organization and that it needs to happen quickly. There may be little awareness of this need in the organization or, alternatively, changes may have already commenced and you can then use the Guide to evaluate existing approaches and find ways in which they can be improved.

The Guide has been developed around the "10 Winning Conditions" for organizational change necessary for success:

1. Correct diagnosis of the change challenge

2. Early development of shared understanding

3. Enrichment of shared understanding

4. A sense of urgency

5. A limited and focused strategic agenda

6. Rapid strategic decision-making and deployment

7. A human flywheel of commitment

8. Identification and management of sources of resistance

9. Follow-through on changing organization enablers

10. Demonstrated leadership

In addition, the Guide is based on a number of proven principles:

❑ There is no single recipe for success—no "silver bullet."

❑ A sound strategic planning process is the vehicle for driving change efforts.

❑ Successful organizational change requires speed and momentum.

The Guide commences with a section intended to ensure that a focused strategic plan exists. Section 1 is based upon chapter 3 of the book, "Taking Action." The initial activity in this section is a ten-point assessment of the organization's current strategic planning process. This is followed by section 2, which provides the user with an opportunity to define the organizational change challenge. Section 3 is focused on describing how the ten winning conditions can be established. This section should be used in conjunction with chapter 2 of the book, "Establishing the Winning Conditions." Sections 4 and 5 provide a framework for developing initial 100- and 200-day action plans.

SECTION 1

Designing and Leading the Process

❏   **Strategic Planning Process**

❏   **Rapid Decision Making**

❏   **Update and Review**

Is your strategic planning process appropriate?

(This assessment should be completed and discussed by the entire senior leadership team)

A focused and responsive strategic planning process forms the basis for defining and managing rapid organizational change.

Scoring Key (5 = strongly agree; 4 = agree; 3 = unsure; 2 = disagree; 1 = strongly disagree)

1. The process is understood by all key participants. ☐

2. The process is clearly differentiated from operational planning. ☐

3. The level of employee involvement is appropriate. ☐

4. The process includes a comprehensive assessment of the change challenge as well as the basics of macro, industry and competitive environment. ☐

5. There is an appropriate level of formal, informal and ad hoc activity. ☐

6. There are ongoing, periodic reviews of progress. ☐

7. The process is perceived to be creative (enabling). ☐

8. The process focuses on the "make-or-break" issues and opportunities. ☐

9. We obtain "bang-for-our-buck" in terms of the effort invested in the process. ☐

10. The resulting plan is a living, useful document. ☐

Total score (maximum 50) ☐

Total score: _____

Items with a score of either 1 or 2:

_____

_____

_____

_____

_____

_____

_____

_____

Areas for improvement:

_____

_____

_____

_____

_____

_____

_____

_____

Your Strategic Plan

A good strategic plan clearly articulates what the vision is for the organiza-

tion and how that vision will be realized. The key is to clearly link the vision

to tangible tactical action planning. An example is provided on page 9 and

pages 10–17 provide details for each component piece. See chapter 3, "Tak-

ing Action," for additional detail.

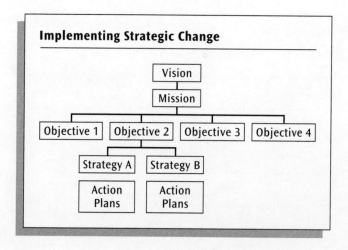

Recall:

Vision: The vision statement is usually for a 3-, 5-, or 10-year period.

Mission: The initial mission usually covers a period of 12–18 months

Strategic objectives: What you wish to achieve during the next 12–36 months

Strategic thrusts: Key initiatives, typically requiring 12 months or more to implement

Action plans: Short-term tactics required to put strategic thrusts into effect over the first 100 and 200 days

---

From Vision to Action Plans

Objective:		Reduce operating cost 15%
Strategic Thrust:		Implement cost management activity
Action:	What:	Cost management workshops for executives
	How:	Get consultant to organize
	Who:	Director General
	When:	Within one month
	How much:	$5,000
Action:	What:	Provide information on cost drivers
	How:	Task force to identify key drivers
	Who:	Director of Finance
	When:	Within three months
	How much:	$5,000

What we want to become: Vision

A good vision statement provides the organization with a clear sense of the long-term direction and purpose for the organization. "Long-term" refers to the limit of your strategic horizon. A good vision statement provides a sense of what the organization is to become, the scope of its activities, and what it will achieve for its key stakeholders.

Our Vision
❏ What we wish to become in concrete terms
❏ Scope of activities
❏ Key points of differentiation
❏ Core values and behaviors
❏ Stakeholder outcomes
❏ Vision time frame

Timeframe: _____

What we wish to become:

_____

_____

_____

Scope of activities:

_____

_____

_____

Key points of differentiation:

_____

_____

_____

Core values and behaviors:

_____

_____

_____

Stakeholder outcomes:

_____

_____

Creating the initial strategic platform: Mission

This framework helps you to define the key elements of your organization's future mission for the next strategic time period.

❏ *Its purpose:* What do we have to deliver in this time?

❏ *Unique identity:* How do we create value for our stakeholders?

❏ *Core values:* What are our 4–5 central beliefs?

❏ *Stakeholder benefits:* What do our owners, employees and customers gain?

Our Mission

❏ Our purpose
❏ Our unique identity
❏ Our core values and behaviors
❏ Our stakeholder benefits
❏ Mission time frame

Timeframe: _____

Our purpose:

_____

_____

_____

_____

_____

Our unique identity:

_____

_____

_____

_____

_____

Core values and behaviors we need to establish:

_____

_____

_____

_____

_____

Key stakeholder benefits:

_____

_____

_____

_____

_____

A limited, focused agenda: Objectives

This framework allows you to identify the four or five key "SMART" objec-

tives for your organization during the next two to three years. What do you

want to achieve in specific, measurable, actionable, realistic, and time-framed

terms? (e.g., 20% unit cost reduction, 100% defect-free deliveries, etc.).

Four or five key strategic objectives sought:

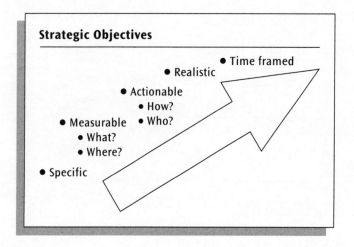

Objective 1:

_____

_____

Timeframe:

_____

Objective 2:

_____

_____

Timeframe:

_____

Objective 3:

_____

_____

Timeframe:

_____

Objective 4:

_____

_____

Timeframe:

_____

Sound action plans

Effective execution requires that good action plans are in place for key initiatives. Employees should be aware of what is to be done within the next 100 days, when, and who is accountable.

Action Plan Structure

Objective:	⬆ Increase market share five points	
Strategic Thrust:	Develop brand extension	
Action:	*Who:*	Product Manager
	What:	Market research—characteristics
	How:	Focus-groups, in-store surveys
	When:	Within three months
	How much:	$50,000
Action:	*Who:*	Product Development Director
	What:	Develop new brand concepts
	How:	Build on market research/project team
	When:	Within six months
	How Much:	$150,000

What is good about our action plans?

_____

_____

_____

_____

_____

_____

What is not-so-good about our action plans?

_____

_____

_____

_____

_____

_____

Where can our action planning be improved?

_____

_____

_____

_____

_____

_____

Effective update and review processes

Effective organizational change requires a periodic assessment of how the process is proceeding, what is being achieved, and what remains to be done.

---

100 Day Implementation Review
10 Key Questions

---

1. How do we feel about the strategy?
2. What are our achievements?
3. What has been accomplished?
4. What are the substantive issues?
5. What are the process issues?
6. How are we doing against our time line?
7. What are our next three months' priorities?
8. What are our next three months' goals?
9. What are our next three months' action plans?
10. What could get in our way?

Are there periodic reviews of our progress built into the process?

_____

_____

Who will attend?

_____

_____

Will accomplishments and achievements be reviewed and celebrated?

_____

_____

Will problem areas be identified?

_____

_____

Will goals and action plans be clearly defined for the next time period?

_____

_____

Will corrective actions be taken when necessary?

_____

_____

Will people be held accountable for their results?

_____

_____

Will peer pressure be used appropriately and effectively?

_____

_____

SECTION 2

Diagnosing the Change

❑   Leading indicators

❑   Depth and breadth of change

❑   Stakeholder analysis

❑   Balance of forces

Recognizing the need for change

The need for significant change can often be masked by strong operating results. However, signals can usually be detected that indicate strategic change is required. These signals are called *leading indicators*. They should be tracked and measured.

Signals for Change Come from:

- ❏ The marketplace
- ❏ Customers
- ❏ Distribution channels
- ❏ Competition
- ❏ Financials
- ❏ Employees
- ❏ Investors

Are strategic change signals coming from:

The marketplace (loss of share, key accounts, etc.):

_____

_____

Customers (defections, low satisfaction, etc.):

_____

_____

Distribution channels (defections, complaints, loss of exclusivity, etc.):

_____

_____

Competition (gaining share, availability of new products/services, etc.):

_____

_____

Financials (shrinking margins, reduced returns, etc.):

_____

_____

Employees (turnover, morale, productivity, etc.):

_____

_____

Investors (share price, investment reports, etc.):

_____

_____

Correctly diagnosing the depth of change required

This framework is intended to help you assess what level of change will be required. Usually, as the depth increases, the elements accumulate, so at the deepest level, paradigm, there will be elements of all types occurring simultaneously.

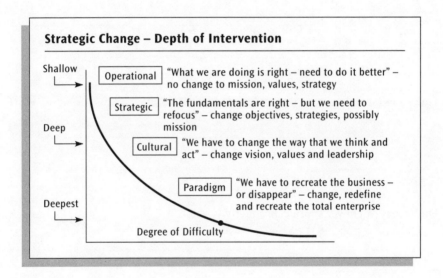

Do we just need to improve what we do?

_____

_____

_____

_____

Do we need to refocus our strategy?

_____

_____

_____

_____

Do we have to change our culture–the way we act and our beliefs and values?

_____

_____

_____

_____

Do we have to change our fundamental business paradigm?

_____

_____

_____

_____

Defining the right tools

This framework allows you to assess whether the right tools are being used to

drive change. Certain tools are more appropriate for certain levels of change.

However, it is important to recognize that as change gets deeper, a broader

array of tools may be required.

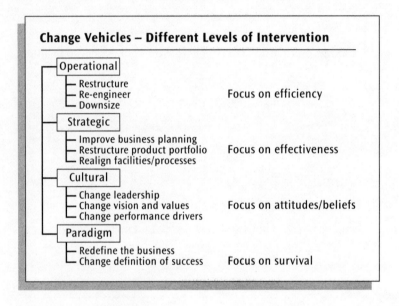

Our level of intervention is:

_____

_____

_____

The appropriate processes and tools are:

_____

_____

_____

_____

_____

_____

_____

We need to change our approach as follows:

_____

_____

_____

_____

_____

_____

_____

Stakeholder analysis

This framework allows you to assess how the change process is perceived by different affected stakeholders. Are they viewing it as positive or negative— or are they unaware of its existence?

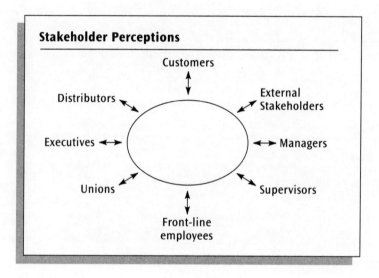

Stakeholder Perceptions

Customers

Distributors

External Stakeholders

Executives

Managers

Unions

Supervisors

Front-line employees

Key stakeholders who either affect or are affected by organizational change:

_____

_____

_____

Stakeholder group	How affected?	Current perception	Impact on outcome

Balance of forces assessment

To bring about change rapidly, key constraints and opposing forces have to be identified and either eliminated or neutralized. This framework allows you to summarize what is needed to overcome these.

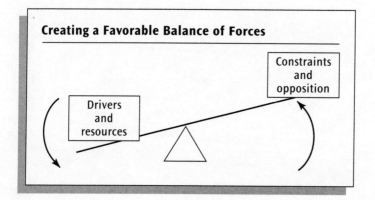

Creating a Favorable Balance of Forces

Drivers and resources

Constraints and opposition

Most important constraints and opposing forces	Current balance of forces (comments)	What is needed to shift the balance
External:		
1.		
2.		
3.		
4.		
5.		
6.		
Internal:		
1.		
2.		
3.		
4.		
5.		
6.		

Definition of the change challenge

This assessment is intended to summarize the nature and scope of the changes required.

> **Strategic Challenge Assessment**
> ❑ Has the correct diagnosis been made?
> ❑ Is the new strategy viable?
> ❑ Are we using the right tools?
> ❑ What is going well?
> ❑ What is impeding process?

Has the correct diagnosis been made?

_____

_____

Is the existing strategy viable?

_____

_____

Are we using the right tools?

_____

_____

_____

What is going well?

_____

_____

_____

What is impeding progress?

_____

_____

_____

Definition of the change challenge:

_____

_____

SECTION 3

Establishing the "10 Winning Conditions"

❑ **Guidance and Shared Understanding**

- Articulation of the change challenge

- Early development of shared understanding

- Enrichment of shared understanding

❑ **Speed**

- A sense of urgency

- A limited and focused strategic agenda

- Rapid decision making and deployment

❑ **Momentum**

- A human flywheel of commitment

- Identification and management of sources of resistance

- Follow through on changing organizational enablers

- Demonstrated leadership

Guidance and Shared Understanding

Articulation of the change challenge

This summary is intended to allow you to define in broad terms the nature and scope of your change challenge, as you have defined it for the organization.

The Nature of My Strategic Challenge

- ❏ Our organization . . .
- ❏ The context of my challenge
- ❏ The nature of the challenge
- ❏ Key stakeholders
- ❏ Desired outcomes

Our organization:

_____

_____

_____

_____

The context of our challenge (why?):

_____

_____

_____

_____

The nature of our challenge (what?—operational / strategic / cultural /

paradigm?):

_____

_____

_____

_____

Key stakeholders (who?):

_____

_____

_____

_____

Desired outcomes (the end outcomes and deliverables):

_____

_____

_____

_____

Creating a shared understanding of required changes

Allowing employees to gain a clear understanding of what is required of them in the change is key to ensuring acceptance and appropriate behaviors.

Initial Shared Understanding

❑ Involvement in strategic planning
❑ Roadshow—2-way (change seminar)
❑ Creative communication (e.g., video)
  — clear message — what / why / how

What activities are underway to build an understanding of the changes required?

_____

_____

_____

_____

_____

Who is involved in these activities?

_____

_____

_____

_____

_____

Who is excluded?

_____

_____

_____

_____

_____

What improvements are required?

_____

_____

_____

_____

_____

Enriching shared understanding

As the change process unfolds, it is necessary to continually ensure that shared understanding is maintained and enriched. Tools for this include studies, pilots, and experimentation.

Enriching Shared Understanding

- ❏ Studies
- ❏ Experimentation
- ❏ Pilots
- ❏ Benchmarking

What activities are underway to build an understanding of the changes required?

_____

_____

_____

_____

_____

Who is involved in these activities?

_____

_____

_____

_____

_____

Who is excluded?

_____

_____

_____

_____

What improvements are required?

_____

_____

_____

_____

A sense of urgency

Step 1:

Create the change message

It is critical in creating the message to establish logical linkages from vision through mission to specific tactical action plans.

Creating the Message

Vision
–here's where we're going

Mission
–here's what we have to do first—campaign #1

Objectives
–here's specifically what we must achieve in this mission (SMART)

Strategic Thrusts
–here's how we're going to achieve the objectives

Actions
–here's who is going to do what

What is our current message?

_____

_____

_____

_____

_____

How well is it working?

_____

_____

_____

_____

_____

_____

_____

What more could we do?

_____

_____

_____

_____

_____

_____

_____

A sense of urgency

Step 2:

Create awareness of and communicate the need for change

The need for change may not be evident to many employees and stakeholders, especially if operating performance is satisfactory. A first step is to create broad awareness of the need for change.

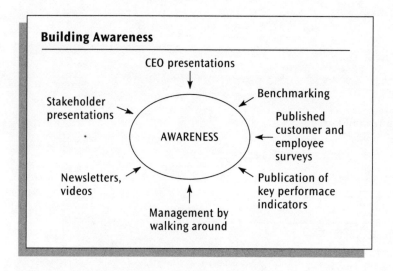

What are we currently doing to create awareness?

_____

_____

_____

_____

How well are we doing it?

_____

_____

_____

_____

_____

_____

_____

What more could we do?

_____

_____

_____

_____

_____

_____

_____

_____

A sense of urgency

Step 3:

Answering the "why" question

It is key to build a powerful rationale for why change is necessary. This is particularly critical when there is no crisis or "burning platform" to galvanize action.

Creating the Change Platform

- ❑ Burning platform: "we'll be out of business if it doesn't work"
- ❑ Sense of competitive spirit: "we need to stay/get ahead"
- ❑ It's going to be fun and rewarding: "there's something in it for you"
- ❑ We're in this together: "you're part of the team, so get with the program"
- ❑ Leadership: "We believe it, so should you"

What is our change platform?

_____

_____

_____

_____

_____

_____

Is it sufficient?

_____

_____

_____

_____

_____

_____

_____

What more could we do?

_____

_____

_____

_____

_____

_____

_____

A sense of urgency

Step 4:

Ensuring powerful symbols exist

In the short term it may not be possible to gain major, significant "wins" to reinforce the need for change. Symbolic actions and results, which may or may not be of strategic significance, are of critical importance. Are you doing enough?

Symbolic Indicators of Change

- ❏ Hire/fire employees
- ❏ Change the slogan
- ❏ Drop products, close facilities—fast!
- ❏ Experiment with new approaches
- ❏ Visible executive actions—walk the talk
- ❏ Informal recognition schemes
- ❏ Physical workplace changes
- ❏ Visible targets, performance measures

What visible, tangible signs of our new direction are perceived by employees and other key stakeholders (e.g., customers)?

_____

_____

_____

_____

_____

_____

_____

What more could we do?

_____

_____

_____

_____

_____

_____

_____

Resourcing key initiatives adequately

These four requirements are key for the effective, rapid deployment of crucial change initiatives:

❏ A limited number of initiatives—speed requires focus and clear priorities.

❏ Adequate resources allocated—momentum requires a critical mass of resources.

❏ A designated champion—ownership of change initiatives is key.

❏ Coalitions/networks—the "human flywheel" is dependent on rapidly mobilizing the "true believers."

Key Requirements

❏ A limited number of key initiatives (2–4)
❏ Adequate resources allocated
❏ A designated champion
❏ Coalition/networks

Is there a limited number of key initiatives?

_____

_____

_____

_____

What resources are available to each initiative?

_____

_____

_____

_____

_____

Who is the designated champion for each initiative?

_____

_____

_____

_____

_____

What supporting coalitions are in place?

_____

_____

_____

_____

_____

Employing a parallel deployment approach

This framework allows you to identify whether organizational change is being deployed rapidly through four parallel streams of activity—symbolic, communication, organization change, and substantive actions—to change the way business is conducted.

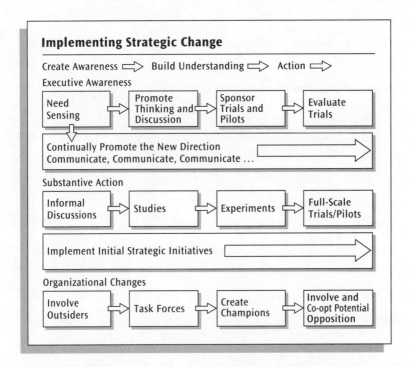

Communication—how are we continually promoting the new direction?

_____

_____

_____

Symbolic activities—how are we demonstrating a new approach?

_____

_____

_____

_____

Substantive actions—what are we changing (e.g., markets, products,

facilities)?:

_____

_____

_____

_____

Organization change—how are we altering the way we do business

(e.g., processes, structure, relationships)?

_____

_____

_____

_____

Momentum

Avoiding the "Valley of Despair"

The "Valley of Despair" may arise for a number of reasons: loss of focus on operations, poor sequencing of change activities, or failure to create a positive environment for change. The key is to avoid the valley.

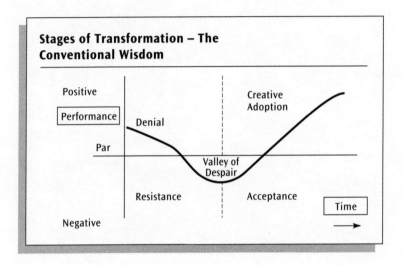

Stages of Transformation – The Conventional Wisdom

Positive

Performance

Par

Negative

Denial

Valley of Despair

Resistance

Creative Adoption

Acceptance

Time

How can we avoid:

Customer service degradation?

_____

_____

_____

_____

_____

Key employees' loss of operations focus?

_____

_____

_____

_____

_____

Change initiatives being incorrectly sequenced?

_____

_____

_____

_____

_____

How can we build a positive environment for change?

_____

_____

_____

_____

_____

Developing the human flywheel

The rate of organizational change depends on the size of the human flywheel and the resulting leverage and momentum that is created. The flywheel will either help avoid, or pull the organization through, the "Valley of Despair."

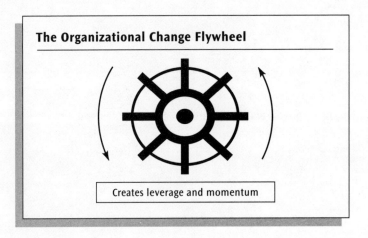

The Organizational Change Flywheel

Creates leverage and momentum

Number of employees in our organization: _____ A

Number of employees *actively* driving change: _____ B

Number of employees *opposing* change: _____ C

Number of employees who could *potentially*

    actively drive change: _____ D

Our leverage ratio: B/A   = _____

Our balance of force ratio: B/C   = _____

Our *potential* leverage ratio: D/A   = _____

Implications for our organization:

_____

_____

_____

_____

_____

_____

_____

_____

Implications for action:

_____

_____

_____

_____

_____

_____

_____

_____

Exploiting the 20:70:10 rule

In most instances, no matter how radical or tough the proposed changes, at least 20% of the employees will be willing to actively support the new direction, 10% will be openly opposed, and 70% will be uncommitted.

20:70:10—The Initial Balance of Forces

❏ 20% of employees will actively support the changes
❏ 70% of employees will remain neutral and/or be perceived to be resistant
❏ 10% of employees will oppose the new direction

Who are the 20%? Are they actively involved?

_____

_____

_____

_____

_____

_____

_____

_____

_____

_____

_____

Who are the 70%? How can they be brought on board?

_____

_____

_____

_____

_____

Who are the 10%? What can be done to neutralize them?

_____

_____

_____

_____

_____

What are the implications of this analysis for our change initiative?

_____

_____

_____

_____

_____

Fully and rapidly engaging employees

There are many ways to gain the active involvement of a broad cross-section of employees in actively driving change. These are some of the ways that the 20% of employees who are "true believers" can be actively involved early in the process.

> ### Involving Employees in Change
>
> ❑ As champions of specific initiatives
> ❑ In task forces, project teams
> ❑ In training activities
> ❑ In feedback sessions, focus groups
> ❑ In benchmarking activities
> ❑ In continuous improvement, idea proposal schemes

Actions required to rapidly engage the 20%:

_____

_____

_____

_____

_____

_____

Current initiatives underway or contemplated to gain broad, *active* involvement:

_____

_____

_____

_____

_____

_____

_____

_____

Opportunities to enhance the level of involvement:

_____

_____

_____

_____

_____

_____

_____

Identifying and addressing barriers

This checklist allows you to identify the most significant barriers to implementation and outline corresponding actions to address them.

> ### Barriers to Change
>
> ❑ "Mooses" or "undiscussables"
> ❑ Key resource limitations
> ❑ Passive or active resistance
> ❑ Lack of motivation/incentive
> ❑ Lack of accountability

"Mooses" or "undiscussables":   Action required:

_____   _____

_____   _____

_____   _____

_____   _____

Key resource limitations: Action required:

_____   _____

_____   _____

_____   _____

Passive or active resistance:

Action required:

_____

_____

_____

_____

_____

_____

_____

_____

_____

_____

Lack of motivation/incentive:

Action required:

_____

_____

_____

_____

_____

_____

_____

_____

_____

_____

Lack of accountability:

Action required:

_____

_____

_____

_____

_____

_____

_____

_____

Utilizing good project management disciplines

Effective deployment of change initiatives requires the use of sound project management practices. This checklist allows you to assess whether you have the key elements of a sound methodology in place.

Key Project Management Disciplines

- ❏ Clear goals and time frames
- ❏ Initiatives thoroughly scoped
- ❏ Leadership/teams in place
- ❏ Effective start-up practices
- ❏ Planning/control software used
- ❏ Post-audits—capture learning

Are key employees trained in project management?

_____

_____

_____

_____

Does each major initiative have clear goals and specified time frames?

_____

_____

_____

_____

Are initiatives thoroughly scoped?

_____

_____

_____

Is a sound planning/control approach in place?

_____

_____

_____

Are project roles clearly defined?

_____

_____

_____

Are post-audits used to capture learning?

_____

_____

_____

Embodying new values in the right behaviors

It is relatively easy when deploying change initiatives for affected employees to espouse the "new" way. What is more critical, however, is that they translate these new attitudes and beliefs into the right behaviors.

The Right Behaviors

- ❏ Identification of a "limited" set of core values
- ❏ Translation of core values into specific behaviors
- ❏ Reinforcement of desired behaviors
- ❏ Build in accountability

Core value: _____

Specific leadership behaviors:

_____

_____

_____

Core value: _____

Specific leadership behaviors:

_____

_____

_____

Core value: _____

Specific leadership behaviors:

_____

_____

_____

Core value: _____

Specific leadership behaviors:

_____

_____

_____

Core value: _____

Specific leadership behaviors:

_____

_____

_____

Is the leadership team prepared to lead?

(This assessment should be completed and discussed by the entire senior

leadership team)

Rapid, effective change demands outstanding leadership qualities.

Scoring Key (5 = strongly agree; 4 = agree; 3 = unsure; 2 = disagree; 1 = strongly disagree)

1. I view change as an opportunity, not a threat. ☐

2. I am willing to listen to a broad diversity of inputs. ☐

3. I am capable of taking a stand—making the tough calls. ☐

4. I can infuse a sense of urgency and enthusiasm into the process. ☐

5. I am firm on what is nonnegotiable. ☐

6. I can adapt my leadership style to the specific situation. ☐

7. I am willing to abandon what is no longer working—no matter
   how familiar. ☐

8. I am willing to challenge conventional wisdom and our assump-
   tions about ourselves. ☐

9. I hold people accountable for results. ☐

10. I am good at recognizing and rewarding appropriate behavior. ☐

Total score (maximum 50) ☐

Total score: _____

Items with a score of either 1 or 2:

_____

_____

_____

_____

_____

_____

_____

Areas for improvement:

_____

_____

_____

_____

_____

_____

_____

_____

Recognizing and rewarding the change leaders

Are employees who are supporting the new approach being recognized and rewarded, or penalized? Failure to change performance evaluation, recognition, and reward systems undermines the process, especially when culture change is required.

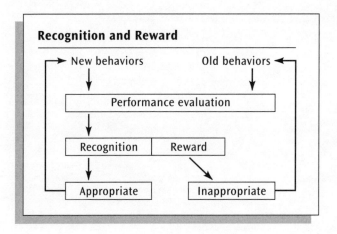

Is there a specific recognition/reward for supporting the new direction?

_____

_____

_____

_____

_____

Is the recognition/reward adequate?

_____

_____

_____

_____

_____

What can we do to enhance recognition/rewards for desired behaviors
and results?

Formal:

_____

_____

Informal:

_____

_____

SECTION 4

The 100-Day Action Plan

In this section of the Guide you will map out *your* plan of action for effectively and efficiently managing the first 100 days of the change your organization is about to or is going through. Using the same framework used for mapping out your organization's strategic plan, you will identify specific objectives, strategic thrusts, and action items to ensure that the 10 winning conditions are established and maintained throughout your change journey. This section will form your game plan for successfully managing change.

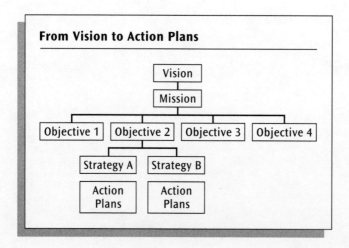

From Vision to Action Plans

Recall:

Strategic objective: What you wish to achieve

Strategic thrust: Key initiatives (how you will achieve the objective)

Action plans: Short-term tactics required to put strategic thrusts into effect

over the first 100 days

Action Plan Structure

Objective:		Create broad stakeholder awareness of need for change within 60 days
Strategic Thrust:		Undertake in-person CEO Roadshow across country—½-day sessions, each city, all employees, management/supervisor
Action:	*What:*	Create multimedia presentation
	How:	Consulting firm to assist
	Who:	CEO/EA
	When:	Within two weeks
	How much:	$10K
Action:	*What:*	Organize and complete tour
	How:	Consulting firm to assist
	Who:	CEO/EA
	When:	Within 60 days
	How Much:	$50K

Our Change Mission:

_____

_____

_____

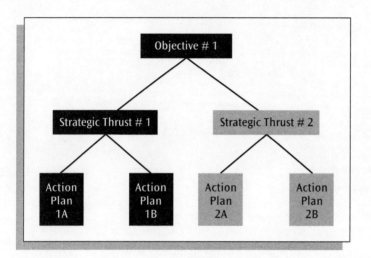

Objective # 1:

_____

_____

Strategic Thrust # 1:

_____

_____

Action Plan 1A:

What (specific objectives and deliverables): _____

How: _____

Who: _____

When: _____

Budget: _____

Action Plan 1B:

What (specific objectives and deliverables): _____

How: _____

Who: _____

When: _____

Budget: _____

Action Plan 1C:

What (specific objectives and deliverables): _____

How: _____

Who: _____

When: _____

Budget: _____

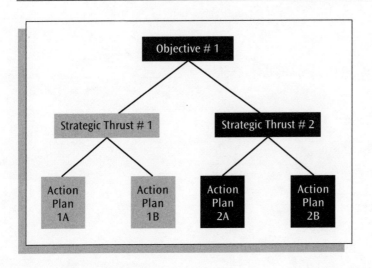

Strategic Thrust #2:

_____

_____

_____

_____

_____

Action Plan 2A:

What (specific objectives and deliverables): _____

How: _____

Who: _____

When: _____

Budget: _____

Action Plan 2B:

What (specific objectives and deliverables): _____

How: _____

Who: _____

When: _____

Budget: _____

Action Plan 2C:

What (specific objectives and deliverables): _____

How: _____

Who: _____

When: _____

Budget: _____

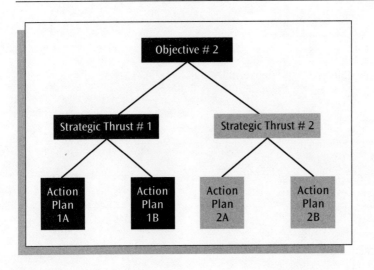

Objective # 2:

_____

_____

_____

_____

_____

Strategic Thrust # 1:

_____

_____

_____

_____

_____

Action Plan 1A:

What (specific objectives and deliverables): _____

How: _____

Who: _____

When: _____

Budget: _____

Action Plan 1B:

What (specific objectives and deliverables): _____

How: _____

Who: _____

When: _____

Budget: _____

Action Plan 1C:

What (specific objectives and deliverables): _____

How: _____

Who: _____

When: _____

Budget: _____

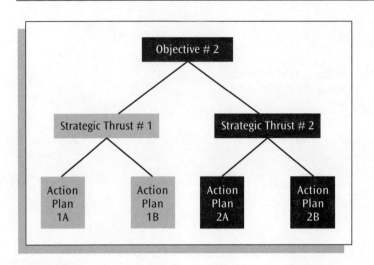

Strategic Thrust # 2:

_____

_____

_____

_____

_____

Action Plan 2A:

What (specific objectives and deliverables): _____

How: _____

Who: _____

When: _____

Budget: _____

Action Plan 2B:

What (specific objectives and deliverables): _____

How: _____

Who: _____

When: _____

Budget: _____

Action Plan 2C:

What (specific objectives and deliverables): _____

How: _____

Who: _____

When: _____

Budget: _____

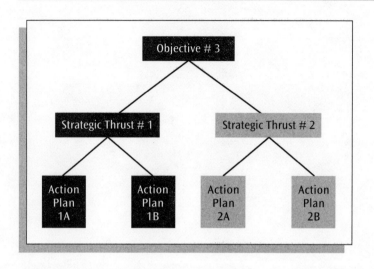

Objective # 3:

_____

_____

_____

_____

_____

Strategic Thrust # 1:

_____

_____

_____

_____

_____

Action Plan 1A:

What (specific objectives and deliverables): _____

How: _____

Who: _____

When: _____

Budget: _____

Action Plan 1B:

What (specific objectives and deliverables): _____

How: _____

Who: _____

When: _____

Budget: _____

Action Plan 1C:

What (specific objectives and deliverables): _____

How: _____

Who: _____

When: _____

Budget: _____

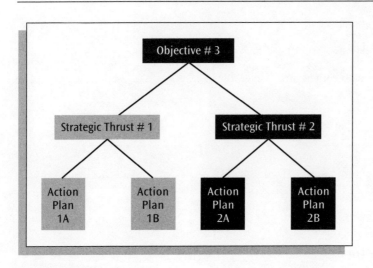

Strategic Thrust # 2:

_____

_____

_____

_____

_____

Action Plan 2A:

What (specific objectives and deliverables): _____

How: _____

Who: _____

When: _____

Budget: _____

Action Plan 2B:

What (specific objectives and deliverables): _____

How: _____

Who: _____

When: _____

Budget: _____

Action Plan 2C:

What (specific objectives and deliverables): _____

How: _____

Who: _____

When: _____

Budget: _____

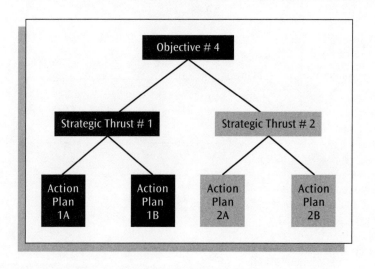

Objective # 4:

_____

_____

_____

_____

_____

Strategic Thrust #1:

_____

_____

_____

_____

_____

Action Plan 1A:

What (specific objectives and deliverables): _____

How: _____

Who: _____

When: _____

Budget: _____

Action Plan 1B:

What (specific objectives and deliverables): _____

How: _____

Who: _____

When: _____

Budget: _____

Action Plan 1C:

What (specific objectives and deliverables): _____

How: _____

Who: _____

When: _____

Budget: _____

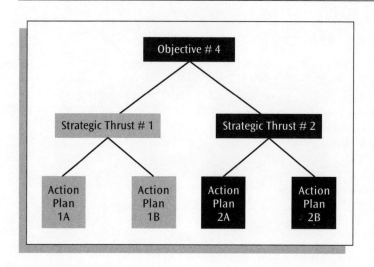

Strategic Thrust # 2:

_____

_____

_____

_____

_____

Action Plan 2A:

What (specific objectives and deliverables): _____

How: _____

Who: _____

When: _____

Budget: _____

Action Plan 2B:

What (specific objectives and deliverables): _____

How: _____

Who: _____

When: _____

Budget: _____

Action Plan 2C:

What (specific objectives and deliverables): _____

How: _____

Who: _____

When: _____

Budget: _____

The First 100 Days Scorecard

The First 100 Days Scorecard is a concise set of measures to enable the leadership team to assess deployment progress. A significant dimension for this scorecard is speed, since this is a major focus for this period. Specific deliverables should be identified, and what is going well and what is not going well should be captured.

The First 100 Days Score Card

❏ Achievement of objectives
❏ Accomplishment of tangible deliverables
❏ Rate of progress
❏ Awareness and communication
❏ Degree of involvement

How well have our objectives been achieved?

_____

_____

_____

_____

_____

What else of significance has been accomplished?

_____

_____

_____

What is going well?

_____

_____

_____

What is not going well?

_____

_____

_____

What are the implications for the second 100 days?

_____

_____

_____

SECTION 5

The Second 100 Days Action Plan

In this section of the Guide you will map *your* plan of action for effectively and efficiently managing the second 100 days of the change your organization is about to or is going through. Using the same framework used for mapping your organization's strategic plan, you will identify specific objectives, strategic thrusts, and action items to ensure that the 10 winning conditions are established and maintained throughout your change journey. This section will form your game plan for successfully managing change.

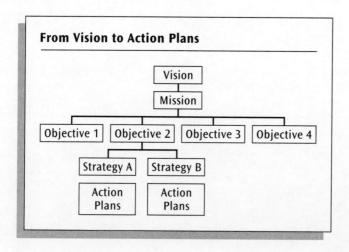

From Vision to Action Plans

Vision
Mission
Objective 1 · Objective 2 · Objective 3 · Objective 4
Strategy A · Strategy B
Action Plans · Action Plans

Recall:

Strategic objective: What you wish to achieve

Strategic thrust: Key initiatives (how you will achieve the objective)

Action plans: Short-term tactics required to put strategic thrusts into effect

over the first 100 days.

Action Plan Structure

Objective:	Create broad stakeholder awareness of need for change within 60 days
Strategic Thrust:	Undertake in-person CEO Roadshow across country—½-day sessions, each city, all employees, management/ supervisor

Action:
What: Create multimedia presentation
How: Consulting firm to assist
Who: CEO/EA
When: Within two weeks
How much: $10K

Action:
What: Organize and complete tour
How: Consulting firm to assist
Who: CEO/EA
When: Within 60 days
How Much: $50K

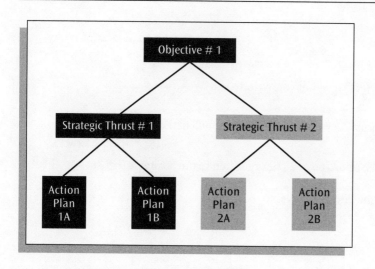

Our Change Mission:

Objective # 1:

_____

_____

_____

_____

Strategic Thrust # 1:

_____

_____

_____

_____

Action Plan 1A:

What (specific objectives and deliverables): _____

How: _____

Who: _____

When: _____

Budget: _____

Action Plan 1B:

What (specific objectives and deliverables): _____

How: _____

Who: _____

When: _____

Budget: _____

Action Plan 1C:

What (specific objectives and deliverables): _____

How: _____

Who: _____

When: _____

Budget: _____

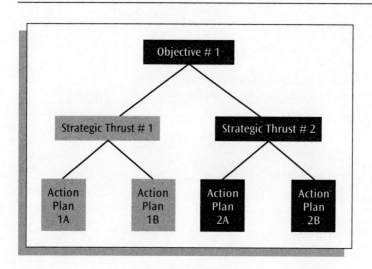

Strategic Thrust # 2:

_____

_____

_____

_____

_____

Action Plan 2A:

What (specific objectives and deliverables): _____

How: _____

Who: _____

When: _____

Budget: _____

Action Plan 2B:

What (specific objectives and deliverables): _____

How: _____

Who: _____

When: _____

Budget: _____

Action Plan 2C:

What (specific objectives and deliverables): _____

How: _____

Who: _____

When: _____

Budget: _____

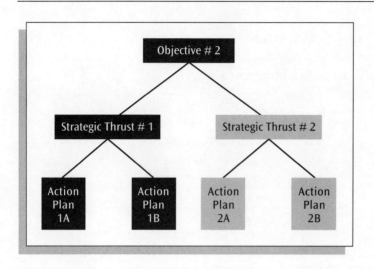

Objective # 2:

_____

_____

_____

_____

Strategic Thrust # 1:

_____

_____

_____

_____

Action Plan 1A:

What (specific objectives and deliverables): _____

How: _____

Who: _____

When: _____

Budget: _____

Action Plan 1B:

What (specific objectives and deliverables): _____

How: _____

Who: _____

When: _____

Budget: _____

Action Plan 1C:

What (specific objectives and deliverables): _____

How: _____

Who: _____

When: _____

Budget: _____

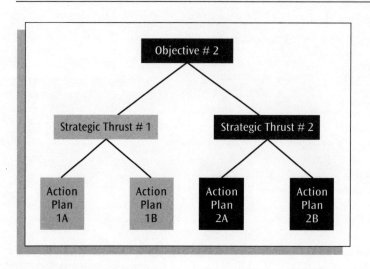

Strategic Thrust # 2:

_____

_____

_____

_____

_____

Action Plan 2A:

What (specific objectives and deliverables): _____

How: _____

Who: _____

When: _____

Budget: _____

Action Plan 2B:

What (specific objectives and deliverables): _____

How: _____

Who: _____

When: _____

Budget: _____

Action Plan 2C:

What (specific objectives and deliverables): _____

How: _____

Who: _____

When: _____

Budget: _____

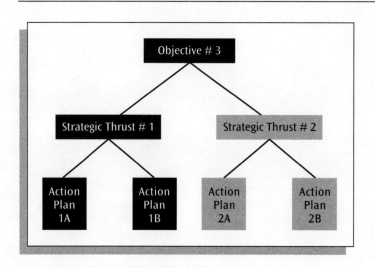

Objective #3:

_____

_____

_____

_____

Strategic Thrust # 1:

_____

_____

_____

_____

Action Plan 1A:

What (specific objectives and deliverables): _____

How: _____

Who: _____

When: _____

Budget: _____

Action Plan 1B:

What (specific objectives and deliverables): _____

How: _____

Who: _____

When: _____

Budget: _____

Action Plan 1C:

What (specific objectives and deliverables): _____

How: _____

Who: _____

When: _____

Budget: _____

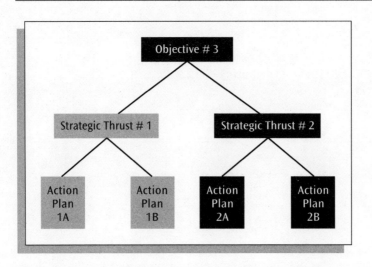

Strategic Thrust # 2:

_____

_____

_____

_____

_____

Action Plan 2A:

What (specific objectives and deliverables): _____

How: _____

Who: _____

When: _____

Budget: _____

Action Plan 2B:

What (specific objectives and deliverables): _____

How: _____

Who: _____

When: _____

Budget: _____

Action Plan 2C:

What (specific objectives and deliverables): _____

How: _____

Who: _____

When: _____

Budget: _____

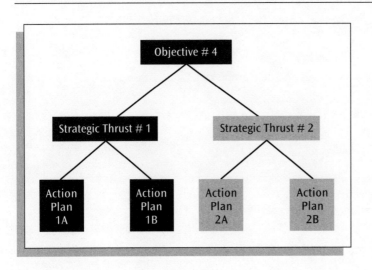

Objective # 4:

_____

_____

_____

_____

Strategic Thrust # 1:

_____

_____

_____

_____

Action Plan 1A:

What (specific objectives and deliverables): _____

How: _____

Who: _____

When: _____

Budget: _____

Action Plan 1B:

What (specific objectives and deliverables): _____

How: _____

Who: _____

When: _____

Budget: _____

Action Plan 1C:

What (specific objectives and deliverables): _____

How: _____

Who: _____

When: _____

Budget: _____

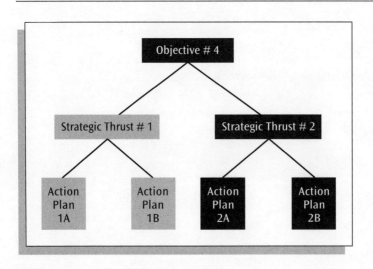

Strategic Thrust # 2:

_____

_____

_____

_____

_____

Action Plan 2A:

What (specific objectives and deliverables): _____

How: _____

Who: _____

When: _____

Budget: _____

Action Plan 2B:

What (specific objectives and deliverables): _____

How: _____

Who: _____

When: _____

Budget: _____

Action Plan 2C:

What (specific objectives and deliverables): _____

How: _____

Who: _____

When: _____

Budget: _____

The Second 100 Days Scorecard

The Second 100 Days Scorecard captures what has been achieved, what's going well, and what's not going well. However, this scorecard is also concerned with momentum since that is the focus of the second 100 days. Is momentum building? Is the human flywheel developing? Are change leaders being adequately recognized and rewarded?

The Second 100 Days Score Card

❏ Achievement of objectives
❏ Accomplishment of tangible deliverables
❏ Momentum of key initiatives
❏ Size of human flywheel
❏ Extent of rewards and recognition

How well have our objectives been achieved?

_____

_____

_____

What else of significance has been accomplished?

_____

_____

_____

What is going well?

_____

_____

_____

What is not going well?

_____

_____

_____